Guide to Sources for Family History held by Westminster City Archives

by

Elizabeth Cory

City of Westminster Archives Centre

City of Westminster Archives Centre

10 St Ann's Street
London
SW1P 2XR

Tel: 0171 641 5180
Fax: 0171-641 5179

© 1997

ISBN 1-900893-03-7

Acknowledgement: *We are grateful to The Grey Coat Hospital for permission to reproduce the photograph on the front cover and to St Stephen, Rochester Row, for permission to reproduce the baptism register from St Andrew, Ashley Place.*

Contents

List of Illustrations

Introduction

Family history needs no introduction. It has become as popular as gardening. If you are new to it, you will soon find out that it is something anyone can do. Indeed many people get completely hooked on it.

This is not a guide to doing your family tree. If you need to know how to start, read one of the many excellent books which have been published on the subject. This booklet is to help you with the sources at Westminster City Archives. It includes details of the sort of information they provide which may be helpful in your research.

Many records about Westminster are at the London Metropolitan Archives (the former Greater London Record Office). The London Metropolitan Archives has all the county and metropolitan records and most of the London parish registers. The Guildhall Library has the Diocese of London administrative records and the parish registers for the City of London.

Most national records for England and Wales are held in central London. These include: post-1837 civil registers of births, marriages and deaths; post-1858 wills; the Prerogative Court of Canterbury (PCC) wills; nonconformist registers; census returns over 100 years old for the whole of England and Wales. The post-1858 wills are at Somerset House. All the other records mentioned in this paragraph are at the Family Records Centre.

Westminster first became a city in 1540, but Westminster City Council was not established until 1900. Prior to 1900 the City of Westminster was comprised of the following civil parishes: St Anne, Soho; St Clement Danes; St George, Hanover Square; St James, Piccadilly; St Margaret, Westminster; St Martin-in-the-Fields; St Mary le Strand; St Paul, Covent Garden; the Precinct of the Savoy and the Liberty of the Rolls. (There were other ecclesiastical parishes.) In 1965 the boroughs of St

Marylebone and Paddington were united with the City of Westminster. They had been the parishes of St Marylebone and Paddington before 1900.

Most of Westminster City's records are 18th or 19th century. However, the ones that go back to the 16th century may have unfamiliar writing. Please ask the archivist on duty if you cannot read a particular word, whatever the period of the writing.

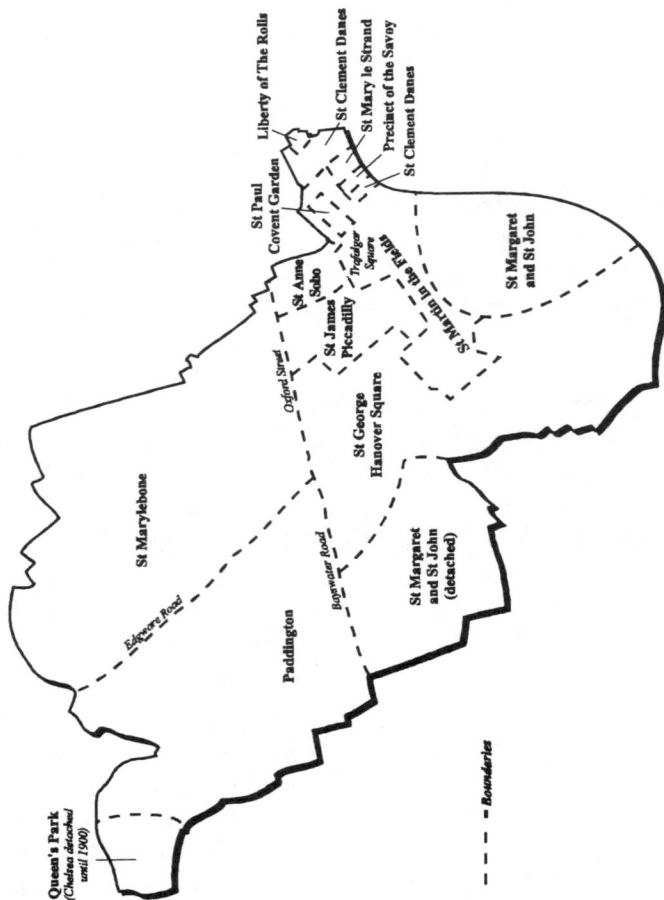

Pre - 1800 Westminster Parish Boundaries

Liberty of The Rolls
St Clement Danes
St Mary le Strand
Precinct of the Savoy
St Clement Danes
St Paul
Covent Garden
Trafalgar Square
St Margaret and St John
St Anne Soho
St Martin in the Fields
St James Piccadilly
Oxford Street
St George Hanover Square
St Marylebone
Bayswater Road
St Margaret and St John (detached)
Edgware Road
Paddington
Queen's Park (Chelsea detached until 1900)
- - - Boundaries

1. Census returns

Copies of the 1841, 1851, 1861, 1871, 1881 and 1891 censuses for the whole of Westminster are available on microfilm or fiche. The 1841 census for Paddington and the 1861 census for the Pimlico and Belgravia parts of Westminster have not survived.

The censuses are indexed by street. The 1851 census is indexed by surname on microfiche. A surname index for the whole of England and Wales is available on microfiche for the 1881 census.

Censuses are the only documents which list all the members of the family including children and servants. Everyone who was at that address on the night of the census is listed.

Information given:- name, relationship to head of family, marital condition, sex, age, occupation, place of birth (often the parish if in London, otherwise possibly only the county). The 1841 census has ages rounded down to the nearest 5 years and has no specific place of birth, only in or out of the county.

In addition 1821 and 1831 censuses giving one name per household and a statistical breakdown are available for St Marylebone.

2. Original parish registers

Parish registers from 1551 to the 20th century are available only for the old City of Westminster, not St Marylebone and Paddington. See *Information Sheet 1: Parish Registers*. Any indexes available here are noted on the list in the search room. Most St Marylebone and Paddington parish registers are held at the London Metroplitan Archives.

Baptism registers usually give the parents' names and sometimes the child's date of birth. From 1813 onwards they give the name, parents' names, address, father's occupation, officiating minister and sometimes the date of birth of the child. Baptism registers do not give the mother's maiden surname.

When Baptized.	Child's Christian Name.	Parents' Name. Christian.	Parents' Name. Surname.	Abode.	Quality, Trade, or Profession.	By whom the Ceremony was performed.
1861 Feb 7 24 No. 273.	Frederick	Richard & Catherine	Harris	Brewer's Yard	Stableman	W. Tipton
~~Feb~~ March 3 No. 274.	Elizabeth	Matthew & Eliza	Godfrey	24 Castle Lane	Baker	W. Tipton
March 10 No. 275.	Louisa Maud	Joseph & Anna Emma	Cherry	1 Palace Street	Cook	W. Tipton
March 10 No. 276.	Charles William	Charles William & Eliza Eleanour	Hawkes	5 William Street	Smith	W. Tipton
March 24 No. 277.	Arthur Richard	William Henry & Anne	Wall	10 York Place	Servant	W. Tipton
March 24 No. 278.	Susan Elizabeth	Robert & Sarah	Stocker	10 Palace Street	Letter-Carrier	W. Tipton
March 24 No. 279.	Arabella	Joseph & Martha	Goddard	10 York Place	Accouchement Maker	W. Tipton
March 31 No. 280.	Elizabeth	Edward James & Maria	Butler	13 Stockbridge Terrace	Cowman	W. Tipton

BAPTISMS solemnized in the Parish of St Andrew Westminster in the County of Middlesex in the Year 1861

St Andrew, Ashley Place, baptism register, 1861

Marriage registers give the names of the parties and their parish of residence. The father's name is given if the bride or groom is under age. From 1754 onwards they give names, parish, marital condition, name of officiating minister, signatures and witnesses. From 1837 onwards they give names, age (often just "full age" - 21 from 1748 onwards), marital condition, occupation, address, fathers' names and occupations, name of officiating minister, signatures and witnesses.

See also Marriage licences, section 9, below.

Banns registers have no additional information to marriage registers. They do not state addresses, nor parents' names, but merely record the parish(es) of the couple and the dates of the calling of the banns. They are only of use to trace a marriage which might have taken place in another parish.

Burial registers give the name and usually whether man, woman or child (M, W or C). They sometimes give the age, occupation, address or next of kin. From 1813 onwards they give the name, address, date of burial, age and officiating minister.

After 1853 burials were not carried out in central London. See also Cemetery registers, section 4, below.

3. Nonconformist and Roman Catholic registers

Registers for a limited number of nonconformist churches have been deposited.

Photocopies of some Roman Catholic registers, duplicates of those at the Society of Genealogists, are available here.

For full details see *Information Sheet 2: Nonconformist and Roman Catholic Registers.*

4. Cemetery registers

Hanwell Cemetery registers, 1867-1949 and 1965-1981 are available. Those for 1905-1914 are indexed.

St Marylebone Cemetery registers 1930-1963 and other cemetery records for St Marylebone 1855-1990, Mill Hill 1949-1987 and Willesden Lane 1939-1950 cemeteries have been deposited at Westminster City Archives.

To find out about other cemetery registers for the City of Westminster, consult the Society of Genealogists' publication *Greater London Cemeteries and Crematoria.*

Consecration of Marylebone New Burial Ground, at East End Road, Finchley, 1855

5. Trade directories

These cover central London. A nearly complete series of directories from 1736-1991 is available. The Guildhall Library's collection up to 1899 is available on microfilm. There are two series of local directories covering St Marylebone and Paddington from the mid-19th century to the mid-20th century.

A collection of Boyle's Court Guides, Royal Blue Books and Royal Kalendars is available, covering many of the years from 1792-1940.

Directories up to 1816 have alphabetical lists of names only. From 1817 onwards odd years do contain street directories. From 1838 the principal separate sections of Kelly's Directories are streets, commercial (tradesmen listed alphabetically), trades (tradesmen listed by profession), and court (people of social standing listed alphabetically). Boyle's Court Guides have street directories from as early as 1792 as well as the court section listing gentry. Royal Kalendars are useful for looking up civil servants.

6. Rate books

Rate books can be used to establish how long someone was resident at a particular address.

When available, directories should be consulted first to narrow down the period of search in the rate books.

Rate books are often available from the date of building or first occupation of the street. They start in the 16th century for some areas of Westminster. Before 1900 they are arranged by parish and ward (ie district of the parish). There is an index by street which states which parish and ward to check. There are separate lists of rate books available for each parish. There is no street index to the Paddington rate books.

Only one set of ratebooks every 10 years is extant for the parish and metropolitan borough of Paddington from 1860 - 1910. Apart from this virtually all the rate books have survived, making this one of the most reliable sources we have.

There is a separate street index to post-1900 Westminster City Council rate books for south Westminster. Rate books from 1969/70 onwards are not available for consultation because of the Data Protection Act. Rate books from 1972 are at Westminster City Hall. Only data about the value and address of the property may be consulted.

Rate book showing Conduit Street,
St George Hanover Square, 1728

Many of Westminster's rate books have been microfilmed. The rate books give the names of ratepayers listed by street, and details of the rates paid. The ratepayer is the person paying local taxes and can be the occupier or the owner of the house. Rate books before the mid-19th century do not include street numbers and are usually arranged with the streets in the order in which the rate collector walked round.

7. Electoral registers

These can be used instead of rate books for the 20th century, to establish how long someone was resident at a particular address.

The series of these is incomplete prior to 1900. For south Westminster, the old City of Westminster, the series begins in 1906. The St Marylebone area series begins in 1918. The Paddington area series begins in 1902. There are no electoral registers from the years of the two World Wars.

Women over 30 were given the vote in 1918 and women over 21 in 1928. Remember only British citizens have the right to vote, so other nationalities are not listed.

Electoral registers are arranged by street and do not have name indexes.

8. Deeds

Catalogued deeds in the collection held by Westminster City Archives are indexed by name and street. A calendar of the deeds is available.

The indexes to the Middlesex Deeds Register 1709-1837 are held on microfilm.

The Grosvenor Estate Papers contain many deeds relating to the Grosvenor Estate area of Mayfair, Belgravia and Pimlico. It is necessary to obtain written permission from the Grosvenor Estate before consulting their material.

9. Marriage licences

Some special marriage licences are held for the period 1766-1891. Most of them are for St Peter, Eaton Square.

10. Other parish records

Parish records may contain such sources as apprenticeship indentures, school records, lists of workhouse pensioners, settlement papers, enrolment lists of militia and volunteers, Land Tax returns, bastardy bonds, registers of gravestones and charity records. (Poor Law Union records are at the London Metropolitan Archives.)

11. Wills

The City of Westminster Archives Centre holds wills and administrations 1504-1829 proved in the Commissary Court of the Dean and Chapter of Westminster. These are mostly 16th and 17th century wills. An index is available.

The deeds index also includes some wills. Most Westminster wills are available at other record offices, not at Westminster (see introduction).

Middtx   (39)

Thomas Holles aged 19 Years   upwards   passed as a Vagrant from the Parish of St. Nicholas in the City of Durham upon his Oath saith that he was bound an Apprentice to one Mr. Robt. Cadwall in Merry Gold Court in the Parish of St. Martin in the Fields in the County of Middx Glover & served him as an Apprentice for the Space of two Years that he hath never since he left his sd. Master rented Ten Pounds a Year p. Parish Taxes lived with any Person as a Yearly hired Servt. for the Space of one Year or otherwise gained a Settlemt. in any other Place to his Knowledge or belief—

Sworne the 26. Day of   Thos. Holles—
June 1741. before

Examination of a pauper,
St Clement Danes, 1741

15

12. Business records

The records of some businesses are held by Westminster City Archives. These collections occasionally contain wages/salaries books, lists of employees, details of pensions, etc, for example the Liberty's and Watney's records. Personnel records may be subject to long closure periods.

Business records by their nature may contain information about individuals, eg in order books. The records of Tookey and Garstin, funeral directors, are an especially good example.

13. School records

In addition to those records of parish and charity schools mentioned in section 10, other schools have deposited their records, dating from the 17th to the 20th century, some including registers of pupils, or minute books recording the names of children admitted. These schools include the Green Coat School, The Grey Coat Hospital, Westminster City School, St Marylebone Grammar School and the St Marylebone Charity School.

Tomb of Thomas Bromley, Westminster Abbey

14. Monumental inscriptions

Some transcripts of gravestone inscriptions have been made and some are part of the parish archives. Please ask for *Information Sheet 6: Monumental Inscriptions in Westminster.*

15. Newspapers/obituaries

Westminster and Pimlico News is available on microfilm from 1887 to the present day. This is the only long run of a local newspaper for south Westminster.

There are several newspapers covering the St Marylebone and Paddington areas.

Local newspapers give only erratic coverage of obituaries. They do often give reports on Coroners' Inquests.

The Harleian Society publication of *Musgrave's Obituary* for pre-1800 deaths is available. *The Times* is available on microfilm in both Marylebone Information Library and Westminster Reference Library; it is indexed.

16. Maps

These can show you where the family lived. The 1792-99 and 1819 editions of Horwood's map have street numbers and cover old Westminster and most of Marylebone. The Potter map of the parish of St Marylebone, 3 editions, 1821-32 shows street numbering. George Lucas's maps of Marylebone 1846, 1847, 1849, 1851 and 1862 and Paddington 1846, 1847 and 1855 also show street numbers.

The first 60 inches to 1 mile Ordnance Survey maps date from the 1860's. The 1950's 50 inches to 1 mile edition is the first edition of Ordnance Survey maps to include street numbers.

Another useful series of maps are the Goad fire insurance plans 1888-1960's. These cover commercial rather than residential areas. They show street numbers, usage or type of business and the name of the business for large firms.

17. Published sources

The City of Westminster Archives Centre has an excellent collection of books on the Westminster area. These include a collection of Harleian Society transcripts of registers of London churches. The archives centre holds many national genealogical reference works such as the Phillimore marriage registers for England, the Huguenot Society publications and the British Record Society publications.

The 1992 edition of the IGI, the Mormon microfiche index, for London is available. This contains everyone in the baptism and marriage registers microfilmed by the Mormons (plus some additional names added by people doing their family research). It is arranged alphabetically by surname and then Christian name and then in date order. It gives names, date of christening or marriage and parish name.

Westminster Reference Library, St Martin's Street holds many biographical and genealogical reference works.

Useful books

The City of Westminster Archives Centre has many books on how to do your family history.

Also available are works on how to find sources held elsewhere, including Jeremy Gibson's useful series produced for the Federation of Family History Societies.

T V H FitzHugh, *The Dictionary of Genealogy* (Alphabooks, revised edition, 1988) gives very helpful definitions of sources used in genealogy.

Useful addresses

Family Records Centre, Myddleton Street, London EC1 1UW, (tel: 0181-392 5300). Statutory registers of birth, marriages and deaths in England and Wales since 1837 (formerly St Catherine's House). Census returns for England and Wales for the 19th century. Prerogative Court of Canterbury (PCC) wills, nonconformist registers (formerly Public Record Office microfilm room).

Guildhall Library, Aldermanbury, London EC2P 2EJ, (tel: 0171-332 1863). City of London deposited records including Diocese of London records (parish registers, marriage licences, etc), Boyd's Marriage Index, Mormon index for England and Wales (1994 Addendum to the IGI on CD-ROM), Livery companies' records.

Lambeth Palace Library, London SE1 7JU, (tel: 0171-928 6222). Records of the Archbishop of Canterbury including marriage licences.

London Metropolitan Archives, 40 Northampton Road, London EC1R 0HB, (tel: 0171-332 3820). Records of the former County of Middlesex, the LCC and the GLC and deposited records relating to the whole of London, including non City of London and non City of Westminster parish registers.

Principal Registry of the Family Division, Somerset House, Strand, London WC2R 1LP, (tel: 0171-936 6960). Post-1858 wills admitted to probate.

Public Record Office, Ruskin Avenue, Kew, Richmond TW9 4DU, (tel: 0181-876 3444). Records of central government, including immigration records and records of people in the armed forces.